Heroes
of the
Battlefield

BRIAN AND BRENDA WILLIAMS

heinemann
raintree

To contact Capstone Global Library please call 800-747-4992, or visit our web site
www.capstonepub.com

Edited by Helen Cox Cannons
Designed by Philippa Jenkins
Illustrations by HL Studios, Witney, Oxon, England
Original illustrations © Capstone Global Library Limited 2015
Picture research by Jo Milller
Production by Helen McCreath
Originated by Capstone Global Library Limited
Printed and bound in China by Leo Paper Group

19 18 17 16 15
10 9 8 7 6 5 4 3 2 1

Library of Congress Cataloging-in-Publication Data
Williams, Brian, 1943-
  Heroes of the battlefield / Brian Williams.
      pages cm.—(Heroes of World War II)
  Includes bibliographical references and index.
  ISBN 978-1-4109-8048-9 (hb : alk. paper)—ISBN 978-1-4109-8053-3 (pb : alk. paper)—ISBN 978-1-
4109-8063-2 (ebook : alk. paper) 1. World War, 1939-1945—Biography—Juvenile literature 2. Soldiers—
Biography—Juvenile literature. I. Title.

  D736.W555 2015
  940.540092'2—dc23   2014044912

This book has been officially leveled by using the F&P Text Level Gradient™ Leveling System.

Acknowledgments
We would like to thank the following for permission to reproduce photographs: Alamy: Chronicle/Robert Hunt
Library, 18, Daily Mail/Rex, 39, David Cole, cover (left), 26, DIZ Muenchen GmbH, Sueddeutsche Zeitung
Photo, cover (background), Everett Collection Inc/Courtesy; CSU Archives, cover (right), INTERFOTO, 27,
34, Niels Quist, 41, Pictorial Press Ltd, 25; AP Images, 11, 21, Joe Rosenthal, 17; Australian War Memorial,
13; Corbis, 30, Paul Dorsey, 16, The Dmitri Baltermants Collection, 35; Courtesy of Pete Lutken Jr, 10; Getty
Images: AFP/STF, 6, Galerie Bilderwelt, 12, SSPL/Planet News Archive, 32; Glow Images: Heritage Images/
Art Media, 4; Landov: PA Photos, 36; National Archives and Records Administration, 19; Newscom: akg-
images, 9, 28, Mirrorpix, 24, NI Syndication, 38, O"Gorman NI Syndication, 22, Photoshot, 40, picture
alliance/Archiv/Berliner Verlag, 7; Royal Air Force Museum/RAF Air Historical Branch, 31; Shutterstock:
coxy58, 1; The Image Works: SSPL/Planet News Archive, 37, SZ Photo/Schert, 23; U.S. Air Force photo,
29; U.S. Navy photo by Lt. Erik Reynolds, 20; Wikimedia: National Archives USA, 15, U.S. Army, 14.

The heroes featured on the front cover are Douglas Bader (left) and Audie Murphy (right).

We would like to thank Nick Hunter for his invaluable help in the preparation of this book.

Every effort has been made to contact copyright holders of material reproduced in this book. Any omissions will
be rectified in subsequent printings if notice is given to the publisher.

All the Internet addresses (URLs) given in this book were valid at the time of going to press. However, due to
the dynamic nature of the Internet, some addresses may have changed, or sites may have changed or ceased
to exist since publication. While the author and publisher regret any inconvenience this may cause readers, no
responsibility for any such changes can be accepted by either the author or the publisher.

Contents

Ordinary Heroes

News of war over the radio made people uncertain and fearful of what was to come.

Great Britain's prime minister, Neville Chamberlain, broadcast a speech on the radio at 11:15 a.m. on Sunday morning, September 3, 1939. He told listeners that Britain was at war. They did not know then that World War II would last six long years, until 1945. In a world at war, ordinary men and women became heroes.

TAKING SIDES

In 1939, Britain and France went to war with Germany, after Germany's leader, Adolf Hitler, ordered his forces to invade Poland. Britain and France were allies, bound by a treaty to help the Poles.

GLOBAL WAR

In 1940, German armies overran much of Europe. When Italy joined the war in June 1940, fighting spread to the Mediterranean Sea and North Africa. Italy and Germany formed the Axis alliance with Japan in September 1940. The European war became more of a global conflict when Germany invaded the Soviet Union in June 1941 and Japan launched a surprise attack on the United States' naval base at Pearl Harbor, Hawaii, on December 7, 1941. The United States joined the Allies after the attack.

On this map of the Asia-Pacific war, the arrows show how Japan extended its empire. After the Japanese attack on Pearl Harbor in 1941, the Allies pushed back the Japanese in a series of sea and land battles.

N
W E
S

USSR
(Soviet Union)

Manchuria

Korea

Japan

PACIFIC
OCEAN

Midway Islands

China

Iwo Jima

Hawaii

India

Okinawa

Wake Island

Burma

Taiwan

Guam

Thailand

Philippines

Marshall Islands

French
Indo-China

Tarawa

Malaya

Caroline Islands

Gilbert Islands

Singapore

Dutch East Indies

New Guinea

Solomon Islands

INDIAN
OCEAN

Guadalcanal

Australia

Japanese-occupied

Allies

Major battle zones

Japanese advances to 1942

THE ROAD TO WAR

Adolf Hitler ruled Germany from 1933. He built a strong army and air force in order to establish a new German empire, or *Reich*. In 1938, Germany took over Austria and Czechoslovakia. Other countries in Europe let Hitler have his way, in the hope that this would prevent another European war on the scale of World War I (1914–18). This was called appeasement, but it led Hitler to believe that he was unstoppable. In 1939, Hitler attacked Poland. This time, Britain and France took a stand.

WAR IN THE EAST

Japan had its own plan for expansion. It had invaded China in 1931 to form a new empire in Asia. Japan hoped to end European rule in Asia and control the Pacific.

The German *blitzkrieg* used speed and surprise to overpower Polish forces with infantry, tanks, and planes.

At Nazi rallies, Hitler told Germans that their destiny was to rule Europe.

RACE WAR

Hitler was leader of the National Socialists, or Nazis. They hated democracy, communism, and other systems that favored equality. They believed that Jews, the Slavs of Eastern Europe, and other races were inferior to the Germans. They persecuted these groups and systematically murdered millions of people. An estimated 6 million Jews were killed in the Holocaust—a campaign to wipe out the Jewish race in Europe.

DID YOU KNOW ?

The war in Europe started at 4:45 a.m. on September 1, 1939. A German battleship opened fire on a Polish fort near Danzig. Around 1.5 million German soldiers, with tanks and planes, then invaded Poland, in a battle tactic that became known as *blitzkrieg*, or "lightning war."

THE COST OF WAR

By late 1941, two opposing groups were fighting in the war. The Allies were Great Britain, the United States, the Soviet Union, Canada, Australia, and other nations. On the opposing side were the Axis Powers: Germany, Italy, and Japan.

In total, 57 nations took part in World War II. Before the Allies were finally victorious in 1945, there were an estimated 40 to 50 million deaths, more than in any other war in history.

HUMAN COST

The Soviet Union lost one person out of every 22 during the war, listed as either killed or missing. The United States lost one person out of every 450, the United Kingdom one out of every 150, and Germany one out of every 25. Poland suffered most, losing one-fifth of its pre-war population.

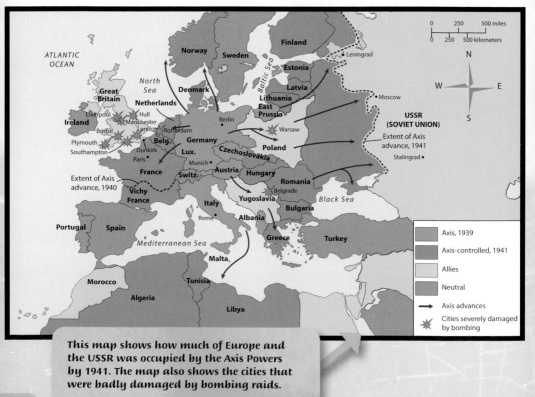

This map shows how much of Europe and the USSR was occupied by the Axis Powers by 1941. The map also shows the cities that were badly damaged by bombing raids.

REAL-LIFE HEROES

War heroes risked their lives every day. Many heroes were just ordinary people who showed extraordinary courage during wartime. Some soldiers were awarded medals, but many acts of heroism went unnoticed at the time, or heroes died on the battlefield, never returning to be honored for their courage.

Battlefield heroes faced new, devastating weaponry and often-terrible battlefield conditions. During the battle for the Russian city of Stalingrad, in the winter of 1942–43, dead soldiers lay in the snow.

HEROES OFF THE BATTLEFIELD

Not every war hero fired guns or flew planes. Millions of people showed courage in their daily lives, doing their best to "carry on" as normal and help others in need.

Soldiers in Combat

Thousands of ordinary people left home to join the armed forces and go to war. After a few weeks of training, they could be sent far away to a strange country, to fight for their lives and those of their comrades.

Pete Lutken

American Pete Lutken (1920–2014) had been outside Mississippi just once before becoming a soldier. Then, in 1942, he was sent almost 9,000 miles (14,500 kilometers) from home to fight in Burma.

U.S. officer Pete Lutken (circled) is shown here with his battalion in 1945.

JUNGLE WAR

In Burma, Allied soldiers fought the Japanese in the jungle. Pete Lutken was on his own as a guerilla soldier, surviving in the thick forests. He raided Japanese camps, blew up railroads, and rescued Allied pilots who had been shot down. He also helped to train local people as soldiers.

TOUGH WORK

The jungle was hot and wet and crawled with insects, bloodsucking leeches, spiders, and snakes. Airplanes tried to drop food and fuel supplies into the jungle, but sometimes the enemy got to the packages first. Many Allied soldiers were so hungry that they had to chew on plant roots to survive.

These are Burmese Kachins helping U.S. troops in 1944. Lutken didn't forget the Kachins, and, once back in the United States, he raised money to build them schools and farms.

JUNGLE RESCUE

It was tricky to rescue wounded soldiers from the jungle—there were few roads, so trucks were not useful. After Lutken was wounded in battle, he had to be carried many miles to safety on a stretcher. Sometimes elephants were used to move supplies around!

FIGHTING FAR FROM HOME

India was part of the British Empire during World War II, so Indian troops fought in Asia and Europe with the Allies. Yeshwant Ghadge was sent to fight in Italy, a long way from his home village near Mumbai.

These are Allied soldiers in Italy at the battle of Monte Cassino, where Ghadge was killed.

ATTACKING A MACHINE GUN

On July 10, 1944, Ghadge was the only unwounded survivor when a German machine gun opened fire on his section of riflemen. Ghadge charged the five-man gun crew. He threw a grenade to kill two, shot a third, and, after running out of bullets, clubbed the last two with his rifle, before he was finally killed by a sniper. He was awarded a Victoria Cross (VC) for his courage.

AN AUSTRALIAN HERO

Australian soldier John French (1914–42) also died to save his comrades. In September 1942, he and his friends came under fire crossing a creek in Papua New Guinea, which Japanese troops had invaded. French told the others to take cover, and he attacked three Japanese machine guns with grenades and a sub-machine gun. He destroyed all three, but his courage cost him his life.

AUDIE MURPHY

Audie Murphy (1925–71) gained more medals for his bravery than any other U.S. soldier of the war—28, including the Medal of Honor, and all by the age of 21. In January 1945, he single-handedly slowed the advance of six tanks and 250 German troops by jumping onto a burning German tank and firing its gun back at them. This gave his men time to regroup and fight back. After the war, he became an actor, starring in Westerns and in a war movie telling his own story.

THE D-DAY INVASION

On June 6, 1944, known as D-Day, the Allies launched a long-awaited invasion of German-occupied Europe. U.S. troops splashed ashore on two beaches in Normandy, France, named Utah and Omaha by the Allies. High above them rose the cliffs of Pointe du Hoc, and hidden there were huge German guns.

Leonard "Bud" Lomell

"I'm the first guy shot in the company, a machine gun through the right side. Then I stepped off into water over my head, and the guys pulled me out and we just rushed to the base of that cliff and grabbed any rope we could get..."

Leonard "Bud" Lomell, on his D-Day experience

On D-Day, 7,000 ships landed an Allied army of 156,000 men in France. It was the biggest seaborne invasion in history.

CLIMB THE CLIFF!

Leonard "Bud" Lomell (1920–2011) and Jack Kuhn were among U.S. Rangers who landed at the bottom of the cliffs. They had the perilous mission of destroying the German guns, allowing Allied troops to land on the beaches. Under heavy fire, they climbed the cliffs using ropes, ladders, and their bayonets to dig handholds.

VICTORY AT A COST

Of the 225 Rangers who scaled the cliffs at Pointe du Hoc on D-Day, 81 were killed and nearly 100 were wounded.

HUNT THE GUNS

By 7:30 a.m., the Rangers had reached the top, but they couldn't see any guns, only a deserted concrete bunker. Eventually, they found them, hidden in an apple orchard. With German soldiers in sight, the pair set off "silent explosives" to wreck the guns. Then, for two days, the Rangers fought off German counterattacks.

A LETTER HOME

Many soldiers didn't tell their families about the dangers they faced every day. In their letters home, they often made it sound like things were better than they really were.

U.S. Marines fought in the Pacific from 1942, starting with the battle for Guadalcanal in the Solomon Islands, and suffered many losses.

FARAWAY FIGHTING

To win the war in the Pacific Ocean, U.S. forces had to drive Japanese troops from their heavily defended island bases. Iwo Jima was one of the last strongholds before Japan itself. On February 19, 1945, 30,000 U.S. Marines landed to fight around 22,000 Japanese, who were ready to die rather than be defeated.

U.S. Marines raise a flag on Mount Suribachi during the Iwo Jima battles of 1945.

WRITING HOME

U.S. Marine Jack Colegrove landed on Iwo Jima. On February 26, he wrote to his mother, telling her he was "without a scratch." Three weeks later, he wrote again to say that he was sorry he hadn't written before, only he'd been wounded. He mentioned a wheelchair. Then he asked a friend back home to tell his mom the real story: he'd lost a leg. In the next letter, Jack told his mother he was "tearing up and down the ward in a wheelchair" and "getting along swell."

A BLOODY BATTLE

The battle for Iwo Jima lasted until March 10, 1945; 6,821 Marines lost their lives, and more than 19,000 were wounded. Only 54 of the Japanese defenders survived to be taken prisoner. The island was just 5 miles (8 kilometers) long, but both sides knew it was a very important step to victory in the Pacific for U.S. forces.

Heroes of the Sea

When HMS *Jervis Bay* (shown here) attacked the *Admiral von Scheer*, Captain Fegen died along with 190 of his 255 crew.

Merchant ships carried important supplies to the warring nations. But a lone merchant ship was easy prey for a submarine or battleship. It was safer for ships to sail in a group, or convoy, with an armed escort.

HMS *JERVIS BAY* ATTACKS

HMS *Jervis Bay* was a British convoy ship, fitted with guns. In November 1940, *Jervis Bay* was escorting 37 merchant ships from Canada to Britain. But, in a nasty surprise, it met a German battleship on the way.

Captain Fogarty Fegen knew his ship could not beat the battleship, but he fought anyway; if he could keep the battleship occupied, the Allied ships carrying essential supplies might escape. HMS *Jervis Bay* was destroyed and sunk, but Captain Fegen's heroism led to 33 ships in the convoy reaching their destination.

PEARL HARBOR

On Sunday, December 7, 1941, Japan launched a surprise attack on the U.S. naval base on Pearl Harbor, Hawaii. Donald Ross (1910–92) was a U.S. Navy machinist (engineer) on the battleship USS *Nevada*. As bombs fell, he knew he must get his ship moving. In choking smoke and scalding steam, he worked alone until blinded and unconscious. After he was rescued, Ross then returned to the inferno to save his ship until he again collapsed. He regained his sight and remained with the USS *Nevada* until the end of the war.

During the battle at Pearl Harbor, about 330 Japanese planes joined the attack. More than 2,388 people were killed, and 21 U.S. Navy ships were destroyed or damaged.

RICHARD McCOOL

Lieutenant Richard McCool (1922–2008) was proud of his little ship.
LCS (L) (3) 122 was a U.S. Navy Landing Craft Support (LCS), known as
a "mighty midget." Big battleships and aircraft carriers fought sea battles,
but the job of an LCS was to provide backup when troops landed in
enemy territory.

HIT BY KAMIKAZE PLANES

On June 10, 1945, McCool's "mighty midget" was in battle off Okinawa.
The little LCS was rescuing men from a sinking destroyer, while kamikaze
planes (see page 21) dived all around. The LCS gunners shot one plane
into the sea, but a second, in flames, crashed into their ship. Badly burned
and wounded, McCool led the fire-fighting and saved his ship and crew.
He was awarded the Medal of Honor for his bravery.

This is LCS (3) 102, another U.S. Navy "mighty midget," just like McCool's ship. Now a memorial to wartime sailors, it is moored in San Francisco, California.

Aircraft carriers were a new weapon in World War II. McCool's LCS would have looked tiny alongside aircraft carriers such as the USS *Lexington*.

BIG SISTERS

Aircraft carriers were a new weapon in World War II and were enormous compared to the "mighty midgets." The biggest sea battles were between aircraft carriers, such as the Battle of Midway between U.S. and Japanese forces in June 1942.

KAMIKAZES

Toward the end of the war, the Japanese used kamikaze pilots. They had one job: to crash their explosives-filled planes into Allied warships, causing maximum damage. Pilots who flew these missions faced certain death.

This is a British midget X-submarine on the surface, with its four-man crew.

SUBMARINE WAR

It was hot, stuffy, and smelly inside a submarine, with 50 men squeezed into a tin tube only about 200 feet (61 meters) long. It was even worse in a mini-submarine.

SINK THE *TIRPITZ*!

British X-craft were mini-submarines only 50 feet (15 meters) long, with four men inside and explosives fixed outside. In 1943, six X-craft launched a daring assault against the mighty German battleship *Tirpitz*, which was lurking in a fjord (a narrow area between cliffs in the ocean) in Norway.

The submarines, numbered *X5–10*, had to find their way underwater through harbor gates and metal nets. *X6*'s captain, Lieutenant Donald Cameron, sneaked in by following a German ship. He released his explosives, but then *X6* got stuck in shallow water. German sailors mistook it for a porpoise! Then they started shooting. *X6*'s crew members were taken prisoner—on the ship they had tried to blow up.

TRAGEDY UNDERWATER

X7 got caught in nets. Wriggling free, it kept bobbing up, then sinking. Lieutenant B. C. Godfrey Place scrambled out before *X7* sank for the last time. With the air almost gone, Sub-Lieutenant Robert Aitken got out through the escape hatch, but his two comrades died.

THE FATE OF *X5*

X5 was never seen again, and the Germans said they sank it. None of the six X-craft that set out on the Norway raid returned home.

DID THE ATTACK SUCCEED?

The attack badly damaged the huge German battleship, which never fought again. *Tirpitz* sailors gave the X-craft survivors blankets and hot drinks. They admired their courage.

The German battleship *Tirpitz* was nicknamed "the Beast."

War in the Air

Fighter pilots had to "scramble" when enemy planes were sighted. Sometimes they had to pull on flying gear over their pajamas.

Much of World War II was fought in, or from, the air. Bombers blitzed cities and fighters fought air battles. Strike aircraft supported armies and navies, and pilots flew secret missions into enemy territory.

DAVID COX

In the summer of 1940, David Cox (1920–2004) was a 20-year-old Royal Air Force (RAF) Spitfire pilot in the Battle of Britain. Germany was preparing to invade Britain from France. By the end of the Battle of Britain in September 1940, Germany had lost 1,773 aircraft, compared to 915 British aircraft. Hitler canceled the invasion, and Britain was safe.

"One got underneath me and there was a flash and a bang and that was it."

David Cox's description of when a German pilot shot his Spitfire and he had to bale out by parachute, landing in a British field

24

FLYING HERO

On September 15, 1940, David Cox was flying alone, which was often risky for a wartime pilot. He spotted six planes. Were they friendly? He flew closer. Black crosses on the wings meant German Me-109s! He shot one down before speeding away.

LUCKY ESCAPES

In a later battle, David Cox was shot down, but he parachuted to Earth with an injured leg. In 1941, his plane crash-landed on a beach. Cox later flew in North Africa, in the D-Day invasion, and ended the war in Asia. He'd been lucky; he had flown through the war and lived to tell the tale.

Douglas Bader

Air forces fought in every war zone, and new pilots had to learn fast, or risk being shot down in flames. Before each mission, fliers wondered whether they would make it back. Many air force crews were very young, with no experience of air war. British pilot Douglas Bader, part of the RAF, was one of the older pilots.

DOUGLAS BADER

Douglas Bader (1910-82) joined the RAF in 1928, but after a plane crash in 1931, he was so badly injured that doctors had to amputate his legs. He learned to walk again on artificial legs and wanted to return to flying, but the RAF refused. However, when war began in 1939, he was allowed to fly again. Bader shot down at least 20 planes in the Battle of Britain, but in 1941, his Spitfire collided with a German fighter over France. He parachuted to the ground, but was taken prisoner. Even in the prison camp, he kept trying to escape.

Billy Fiske

Billy Fiske (1911–40) was an American Olympic bobsled champion who joined the RAF. On August 16, 1940, he flew his damaged Hurricane fighter back to base after battle instead of parachuting out of it. Billy landed, but he was badly burned and died the following day. He was one of the first Americans to die in World War II.

FASTER AND FASTER

In 1939, the fastest warplanes, like the British Spitfire, had a top speed of about 350 miles (560 kilometers) per hour. By 1945, the German Me-262 jet could top 500 miles (800 kilometers) per hour!

27

These are U.S. Navy Wildcats. The pilot nearest the camera is John Thach, a fighter ace who came up with new flying tactics.

MEDIA HEROES

Fighter pilots became war heroes, pictured in newsreels and magazines because people admired their courage in the skies. When the United States joined the war, Joe Foss was assigned to a squadron in order to take photos of the enemy. Foss was desperate to fight, and he persuaded his superiors to allow him to join the U.S. Marine Corps as a fighter pilot. Their decision paid off. In November that year, Foss became the first U.S. fighter pilot to score 20 victories. Flying his Grumman F4-F Wildcat, Foss knew he must never underestimate his Japanese opponent, especially in a nimble Zero fighter. His advice to young pilots was: "If you're alone, and you meet a lone Zero, run like hell—you're outnumbered!"

FIGHTER ACES

Top-scoring fighter aces of World War II included the U.S. Air Force's Dick Bong, who claimed 40 hits, Johnnie Johnson (RAF, 38), David McCampbell (U.S. Navy, 34), and Clive Caldwell (Royal Australian Air Force, 28). None of those compare with German ace Erich Hartmann of the Luftwaffe, who achieved 352 hits.

Lee Archer

Lee Archer (1919–2010) from Harlem, New York City, was one of the first African American pilots to join the U.S. Air Force. After training at Tuskegee, Alabama, Archer flew in combat in Italy, escorting Allied bombers. One day in October 1944, he shot down three German planes. By 1945, he had flown 169 missions in his P-51 Mustang as a member of the "Red Tails" fighter group.

GOOD LUCK NAMES

Lee Archer named his plane "Ina" (after his wife). Many fliers painted their planes with lucky names and symbols.

Bomber Crews

A B-17, like these ones flying over Germany in 1943, had a crew of 10 men and 13 machine guns. This earned the B-17 the nickname "Flying Fortress."

World War II bombers were bigger and slower than fighters. They carried aircrews consisting of pilots, navigators, radio operators, bomb-aimers, and air gunners. The crew fought as a team.

BOMBING DAY AND NIGHT

In the skies over Europe, RAF bombers attacked at night and U.S. bombers attacked by day. Daylight raids were more dangerous, but U.S. pilots believed they could hit their targets more accurately during the day. Most missions lasted many hours; it was freezing cold, noisy, cramped, and dangerous. Many bombers were shot down by fighters or "flak" (German anti-aircraft guns). Most of the 160,000 Allied airmen killed during the war were members of bomber crews.

THE DAMBUSTERS RAID

In 1943, RAF Lancaster bombers raided German waterways in what would become known as the Dambusters raid. Twenty-four-year-old Wing Commander Guy Gibson was personally selected to lead the mission. He'd already made many bombing missions and won medals for his bravery.

The bombers flew low—only 60 feet (18 meters)—above German rivers in order to drop "bouncing bombs" onto dams. Of the 19 Lancasters that took part in the mission, 8 were lost, and 53 men were killed. However, the mission was largely successful, as flooding from the destroyed dams caused damage to many German factories, power stations, and road and rail bridges.

Dambuster leader Guy Gibson is shown with a photo of a dam breached in the attacks.

JUMPING OUT

Aircrew were not always able to use parachutes. George Silva, an air gunner in a B-17, was lucky. Over France, in March 1944, his plane was hit by German gunfire and spiraled down in flames. Somehow, George struggled into his parachute and fell out of the doomed plane as it broke apart. He drifted down among bombs falling from other B-17s. After landing, he became a prisoner of war (POW) and was freed when the war ended a year later.

Special Forces

Some soldiers, including commandos and U.S. Rangers, were trained specifically for the riskiest of missions.

AIRBORNE HEROES

In June 1944, Allied airborne soldiers landed in France to begin the D-Day invasion. Some flew in gliders, many of which crashed. Others were dropped into France by parachute, though many landed way off target. John Steele of the U.S. 82nd Airborne Division landed on a church steeple in Sainte-Mère-Eglise, France. He dangled above the town square for two hours before being taken prisoner.

Wooden gliders, like this Hamilcar, landed Allied soldiers to fight D-Day battles in 1944.

JAKE McNIECE AND THE "FILTHY THIRTEEN"

Jake McNiece (1919–2013) led a U.S. Army unit that was parachuted into France just before the D-Day landings. McNiece was part-Choctaw American Indian. His unit was nicknamed the "Filthy Thirteen" because they only washed once a week and never cleaned their uniforms! The Filthy Thirteen built up a reputation for stealing rations and wrecking jeeps. While they may have broken rules, they were very good at blowing up enemy targets, and McNiece was fiercely brave and hugely respected. The 1967 film *The Dirty Dozen* was based on the unit's experiences.

TANK-FIGHTING AT ARNHEM

In September 1944, the Allies dropped U.S., British, and Polish airborne troops into Arnhem, in the Netherlands. They were hoping to capture bridges on the Rhine River in order to speed up the end of the war. Major Robert Cain and his troops landed by glider and fought off German tanks for almost a week.

Cain was wounded and briefly lost his sight and hearing, but he still managed to destroy six enemy tanks. He and his men escaped by crossing the river in a leaky boat, using their rifles as paddles. However, despite the bravery of the troops fighting in the Netherlands, the attack at Arnhem was a failure.

DID YOU KNOW?

Commandos and U.S. Rangers were so successful in their dangerous missions that Hitler secretly ordered that all captured commandos be shot, without trial, even if they surrendered.

Behind Enemy Lines

These trucks of the Long Range Desert Group in northern Africa are on a raid.

Raids into enemy territory called for skill and daring—and unusual methods. Until his capture in 1943, David Stirling led a band of British desert raiders in northern Africa, where Allied and German forces were fighting. Ralph Bagnold, another British raider, was an experienced desert explorer who'd volunteered to be a "desert pirate." His Long Range Desert Group roamed in trucks across the desert, attacking the enemy.

JUNGLE TRAILS

In the jungles of Asia, however, trucks were of little use. General Frank Merrill led 3,000 U.S. troops (nicknamed "Merrill's Marauders") in a jungle war against a much bigger Japanese army. His men would walk into battle, with only mules to carry supplies. In March 1944, the Marauders marched 100 miles (160 kilometers) to attack a Japanese supply route.

SNIPER WAR

Snipers were both admired and feared. Anatoly Chekhov was a Russian sniper at the Battle of Stalingrad. He hid in a tall building, firing a rifle with a telescopic sight and a cover to hide the muzzle-flash, which might give away his position.

MORE UNUSUAL METHODS

Some people working as British and U.S. spies journeyed to occupied countries in order to help resistance fighters carry out sabotage and assassinations in secret. Their unusual weapons included pen-pistols, poison pills, and lumps of coal that exploded! If they were captured, they faced torture and almost certain death.

Russian snipers lie in wait for a shot at the enemy.

Unsung Heroes

Women in uniform supported fighting men, but few armies sent female soldiers into combat. However, many women risked their lives in war zones. In air raids, they rescued bomb victims and drove ambulances. They worked anti-aircraft guns and searchlights to help fight off enemy bombers. At fighter control centers, they directed pilots to intercept enemy planes, often while under fire.

Women's Auxiliary Air Force (WAAF) recruits were trained to keep enemy bombers away, using blimps.

JOAN DAPHNE PEARSON

Joan Pearson (1911–2000) was a member of the British Women's Auxiliary Air Force (WAAF). When an RAF bomber crashed in her airfield in Britain, she rushed to the burning plane to drag out the injured pilot, just before it exploded. In 1941, she was the first woman to receive the George Medal for bravery.

BAI JINGFAN

Women soldiers in the Chinese army also battled against their Japanese invaders. Bai Jingfan (born c. 1918) was 16 when Japanese soldiers attacked her village in 1934. She left to join the rebels, married, and fought the Japanese for the next 11 years. In 1944, while pregnant, Bai hid in a dirt hole from Japanese soldiers who were hunting her. After they had gone, she gave birth to her baby.

CHILDREN AT STALINGRAD

In the Battle of Stalingrad, fought in the winter, food was scarce, and starving Russians were forced to eat rats and horses. Children stole rations from German soldiers, who in turn forced Russian children to fill their water bottles. This was because a child sneaking down to the river was less likely to be a target for a sniper.

GULYA KOROLEVA

Gulya Koroleva (1922–42) left her family and baby in Moscow, in the Soviet Union, to volunteer as a nurse in Stalingrad. She rescued more than 100 wounded men on the battlefield and also fought in combat, killing 15 enemy soldiers before her own death.

WOMEN PILOTS

Many women pilots transported new planes from factories to combat units. Jacqueline Cochran (1910?–80) led the U.S. Women Airforce Service Pilots. Amy Johnson (1903–41), famous for her record-breaking, long-distance solo flights during the 1930s, flew as a British ferry pilot. In 1941, her plane crashed into the sea and she disappeared.

"NIGHT WITCHES"

In Russia, women pilots flew night-bombing missions. In their slow biplanes, they would cut their engines, so that German soldiers heard only a "whoosh" as they glided in. Then they would drop their bombs, before restarting their engines to fly away again. This gave them the nickname the "Night Witches."

Jacqueline Cochran became a flight captain in the British Air Transport Auxiliary in 1941, training a group of female pilots like these.

> "Those who gave in [to fear] were gunned down and they were burned alive as they had no parachutes."

> "Night Witch" flier Nadezhda Popova

UNEXPLODED BOMBS (UXBs)

Hundreds of bombs fell and didn't explode on impact, but they remained dangerous long after the war. Bomb disposal teams were trained to make UXBs safe. In Britain, almost 600 people were killed dealing with UXBs and mines.

Unexploded bombs remain a menace for years after war. Making this wartime bomb safe, in 1975, required cool nerves and steady hands.

COURAGE OFF THE BATTLEFIELD

Many people were heroic for the courage they showed in dealing with the effects of war away from the battlefield. In 1941, RAF pilot Derek Martin was hunting German submarines in the Atlantic Ocean. After a 12-hour mission, he returned to Scotland, but his plane hit the water and broke up, killing or injuring all 11 of his crew. Martin was so badly hurt that it took hospital surgeons a year to repair his face. He and other injured patients started the Guinea Pig Club, for those who had to receive pioneering plastic surgery treatment for their battle injuries.

What Makes a Hero?

The war in Europe ended on May 8, 1945 (Victory in Europe, or VE Day), and in Asia on August 15 (Victory over Japan, or VJ Day). The war lasted longer than World War I (1914–18), cost more lives, and caused far more destruction.

ALL KINDS OF HEROES

Many heroes did not live to see peace. Josef Frantisek was a Czech pilot who came to Britain and shot down 17 German planes in 27 days during the Battle of Britain, before dying in a landing accident.

Thousands of ordinary people found themselves in extraordinary situations. Grace Golland was 22 when she had to leave her family's restaurant business for war. She served in the British Auxiliary Territorial Service, the women's branch providing support for the British army. She fought through a fire-bomb raid in 1944 while stationed at her anti-aircraft gun.

The Bomber Command memorial in London honors aircrew killed or wounded in air battles.

HM QUEEN ELIZABETH II
UNVEILED THIS MEMORIAL
28 JUNE
IN THE YEAR OF HER DIAMOND JUBILEE
2012

WAR MEMORIES

B-17 crewman Elmer Bendiner wrote in his diary during every mission, so that he wouldn't forget any details. During one raid over Occupied Europe in 1943, he kept hearing bad news from crewmates: "plane in flames...planes falling like a stone..." He scribbled down the time, place, and altitude of every plane that was hit. After landing back in Britain, he noted, "We had been in the air for 8 hours 40 minutes. We had been in incessant [constant] combat for close to 6 hours." Sixty other B-17s had not come home. Because of Bendiner and others' bravery in recording the war as it happened, we have some idea of the dangers they faced.

STORIES THAT LIVE ON

Some war heroes were brave without thinking about the consequences. Others saw the dangers, but still decided to risk their lives to help end the war. Almost none of them would have called themselves heroes; rather, they would have said that they were just doing their duty to their country. But to the generations that follow them, the ordinary men and women who sacrificed their everyday lives to fight in the war are true heroes, and we remember their courage through war memorials, books, movies, and family memories.

Timeline

1938	JANUARY	FEBRUARY	MARCH	APRIL	MAY	JUNE

MARCH 12 Germany invades Austria

1939	JANUARY	FEBRUARY	MARCH	APRIL	MAY	JUNE

MARCH 15 Germany invades Czechoslovakia

1940	JANUARY	FEBRUARY	MARCH	APRIL	MAY	JUNE

APRIL 9 Germany invades Denmark and Norway

JUNE 10 Italy enters the war, declaring war on Britain and France

JUNE 14 Germany takes over Paris

1941	JANUARY	FEBRUARY	MARCH	APRIL	MAY	JUNE

JUNE 22 Germany invades the Soviet Union

1942	JANUARY	FEBRUARY	MARCH	APRIL	MAY	JUNE

FEBRUARY 15 Japan captures Singapore from the British

MAY Japan captures the Philippines from U.S. forces. Australia is under threat from Japan.

JUNE 4–7 Naval battle of Midway in the Pacific is the first Allied victory against Japan

1943	JANUARY	FEBRUARY	MARCH	APRIL	MAY	JUNE

FEBRUARY 2 Germans surrender at Stalingrad, in the Soviet Union

1944	JANUARY	FEBRUARY	MARCH	APRIL	MAY	JUNE

JUNE 6 D-Day landings in Normandy, France

1945	JANUARY	FEBRUARY	MARCH	APRIL	MAY	JUNE

FEBRUARY 19–MARCH 26 U.S. Marines attack Iwo Jima. Manila (Philippines) is liberated.

APRIL 30 Russian army arrives in Berlin. Hitler commits suicide.

MAY 8 VE Day–Victory in Europe Day

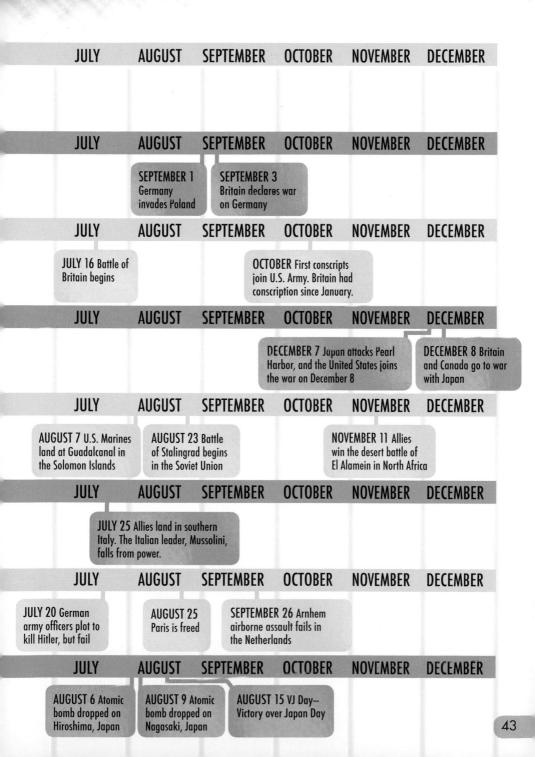

JULY	AUGUST	SEPTEMBER	OCTOBER	NOVEMBER	DECEMBER

JULY	AUGUST	SEPTEMBER	OCTOBER	NOVEMBER	DECEMBER

SEPTEMBER 1 Germany invades Poland

SEPTEMBER 3 Britain declares war on Germany

JULY	AUGUST	SEPTEMBER	OCTOBER	NOVEMBER	DECEMBER

JULY 16 Battle of Britain begins

OCTOBER First conscripts join U.S. Army. Britain had conscription since January.

JULY	AUGUST	SEPTEMBER	OCTOBER	NOVEMBER	DECEMBER

DECEMBER 7 Japan attacks Pearl Harbor, and the United States joins the war on December 8

DECEMBER 8 Britain and Canada go to war with Japan

JULY	AUGUST	SEPTEMBER	OCTOBER	NOVEMBER	DECEMBER

AUGUST 7 U.S. Marines land at Guadalcanal in the Solomon Islands

AUGUST 23 Battle of Stalingrad begins in the Soviet Union

NOVEMBER 11 Allies win the desert battle of El Alamein in North Africa

JULY	AUGUST	SEPTEMBER	OCTOBER	NOVEMBER	DECEMBER

JULY 25 Allies land in southern Italy. The Italian leader, Mussolini, falls from power.

JULY	AUGUST	SEPTEMBER	OCTOBER	NOVEMBER	DECEMBER

JULY 20 German army officers plot to kill Hitler, but fail

AUGUST 25 Paris is freed

SEPTEMBER 26 Arnhem airborne assault fails in the Netherlands

JULY	AUGUST	SEPTEMBER	OCTOBER	NOVEMBER	DECEMBER

AUGUST 6 Atomic bomb dropped on Hiroshima, Japan

AUGUST 9 Atomic bomb dropped on Nagasaki, Japan

AUGUST 15 VJ Day—Victory over Japan Day

Glossary

air raid attack on a target by aircraft dropping bombs

Allies countries, such as Great Britain, France, the Soviet Union, and the United States, that fought against the Axis Powers

amputate remove a limb entirely because injuries are so bad it cannot be repaired

Axis Powers countries, including Germany, Italy, and Japan, that were the enemies of the Allies

Battle of Britain air battle between the Royal Air Force and the German Luftwaffe during the summer and fall of 1940

battleship large warship with big guns

bayonet long knife fitted to a rifle

bouncing bomb bomb designed to bounce across water, then sink and explode next to its target, such as a dam. It was invented by Barnes Wallis, a British engineer and scientist.

breach to break through, due to enemy attack

British Empire countries or territories once ruled over by Great Britain

commando soldier trained for surprise, dangerous raids

comrade fellow soldier or service member

grenade small bomb thrown like a ball

guerilla member of a small, independent group taking part in irregular fighting, often against larger, regular forces

invade when a country attacks another, by sending armies onto its land

Jew person who believes in a form of religion called Judaism

landing craft boat used to ferry soldiers from a ship to the shore

marine soldier who fights from ships

Medal of Honor in the United States, the highest award given for extreme courage in battle

Nazi member of the National Socialist Party in Germany

newsreel program of news films shown at movie theaters, before TVs were available

occupied country that is under the control of another. In World War II, Nazi Germany occupied other countries, including Poland.

persecute treat someone cruelly or unfairly because of his or her race, religion, or political beliefs

prime minister leader of the government in some countries

prisoner of war (POW) someone who is captured by the enemy during war and imprisoned

Ranger U.S. commando-type soldier

resistance groups fighting a secret war against an occupying enemy

rifle long-barreled handgun used by foot-soldiers (infantry)

Royal Air Force (RAF) Great Britain's air force

sabotage deliberately destroy or disrupt something

sniper skilled military shooter who shoots at the enemy from a concealed place

Victoria Cross (VC) in Great Britain and the Commonwealth, the highest award given for extreme courage in battle

Find Out More

BOOKS

Adams, Simon. *World War II* (DK Eyewitness). New York: Dorling Kindersley, 2014.

Atwood, Kathryn J. *Women Heroes of World War II* (Women of Action). Chicago: Chicago Review Press, 2011.

Burgan, Michael. *The World War II Soldier's Experience: An Interactive History Adventure* (You Choose). Mankato, Minn.: Capstone, 2013.

Perritano, John. *World War II: Ten Greatest Heroes*. New York: Scholastic, 2011.

WEB SITES

www.nationalww2museum.org/learn/education/for-students/ww2-history
The National World War II Museum's web site has a useful section full of information written for students.

www.pbs.org/thewar
This is a companion web site to a PBS documentary called *The War*, which explored World War II through people's individual memories and stories.

www.worldwar2history.info/Medal-of-Honor
This web site provides links to the stories behind Americans who received the Medal of Honor in World War II.

PLACES TO VISIT

National World War II Museum
945 Magazine Street
New Orleans, Louisiana 70130
nationalww2museum.org

Smithsonian National Air and Space Museum
Independence Avenue at 6th Street, SW
Washington, D.C. 20560
airandspace.si.edu

FURTHER RESEARCH

We know about World War II from evidence such as books, photographs, movies, radio broadcasts, posters, diaries, and people's memories. Your local public library will have lots of books about the war, some by soldiers describing their experiences in different war zones. Books and online archives are a valuable source of evidence from people who were actually there and who recorded what they saw, what war was like, and how it affected them. See what more you can find about individual heroism in all these places.

Index